T0167195

Angel Cloud Poetry II

Life's Journey

By

David P. Carlson

Order this book online at www.trafford.com
or email orders@trafford.com

Most Trafford titles are also available at major online book retailers.

© Copyright 2014 David P. Carlson.
All rights reserved. No part of this publication may be reproduced, stored in a retrieval
system, or transmitted, in any form or by any means, electronic, mechanical, photocopying,
recording, or otherwise, without the written prior permission of the author.

Scripture quotations marked KJV are from the Holy Bible, King James Version
(Authorized Version). First published in 1611. Quoted from the KJV Classic
Reference Bible, Copyright © 1983 by The Zondervan Corporation.

Printed in the United States of America.

ISBN: 978-1-4907-4661-6 (sc)
ISBN: 978-1-4907-4660-9 (hc)
ISBN: 978-1-4907-4662-3 (e)

Library of Congress Control Number: 2014917213

Because of the dynamic nature of the Internet, any web addresses or links contained in
this book may have changed since publication and may no longer be valid. The views
expressed in this work are solely those of the author and do not necessarily reflect the
views of the publisher, and the publisher hereby disclaims any responsibility for them.

Any people depicted in stock imagery provided by Thinkstock are models,
and such images are being used for illustrative purposes only.
Certain stock imagery © Thinkstock.

Trafford rev. 11/04/2014

 www.trafford.com

North America & international
toll-free: 1 888 232 4444 (USA & Canada)
fax: 812 355 4082

Acknowledgements

By David P. Carlson

Special thanks to Becky Campbell for her consistent support with her many talents that have made these poems artistically legible.

Also, of course, to my wife, Linda, many thanks for her patience and daily encouragements. Without her devotion, love, and faith the inspiration for each poem would have never been manifested on paper.

Finally without my salvation, (provided by the Ancient of Days, God the Father of all the ages, Creator of all that has ever existed) and without the ultimate sacrifice of His only begotten son, Jesus of Nazareth for the sins of all mankind all combined, His mercy, sacrifice and love (these His three essential elements) I would have no reason or compulsion to express any passion worth pursuing --- "all would be vanity".

CORE Sample

By David P. Carlson

In 1953 the Spirit of God drew me out of the pew and into the aisle and down to accept my Lord's salvation. I don't remember what Brother (Rev. Lunsford) said, but I'll never forget the joy of that nine year old boy.

---Nineteen years later---

I often wonder what Brother (Rev. C.C. Hurst) thought that night when the doorbell rang---probably, "Who can that be at this time of night," or "what major problem am I about to face this time?" Hesitantly he opened the door and I heard him say, "Can I help you?" and then, "Oh, David, what's the problem?" I had been at his church before (he immediately recognized sister Bozman's granddaughter's bar-room boyfriend—ME!!) Well, there we were; myself, my girlfriend, and my best friend, J.B White, standing there on the porch. We had been arguing about if God was real over a couple of six-packs (or more maybe). I'm sure he could smell the beer on my breath, but believe it or not, he said, "Let's go over to the church and talk this over. It wasn't long that he cut to the chase and said, "David, do you want ot give your life back to the Lord tonight and receive him as Lord and Savior?" I said, "Yes, Pastor Hurst, I do." I was immediately completely sober. He then led me in the sinner's prayer and that was that. My friend J.B. was stunned, to say the least, and, no doubt, highly disappointed in me. Brother Hurst asked J.B., "How about you son?" J. B. stormed out with an unlit cigarette dangling from his mouth; I think I even heard him curse a little. We had been friends for at least ten years, but everything changed that night. We never really ever spoke again to each other up to the time he died about 15 years later.

Well, I began to display, at that point, a major change. Church was my life and God began to mold me into a new man. I married my girlfriend, (sister Bozman's granddaughter) who had 3 children from former marriages already. Before we married in God's presence, one night he spoke to me to the effect, "I've given you a new life, now will you have a problem with raising these 3 children as your own?" I said, "Yes, Lord, I will do it."

Well, things got better and better. We bought a small trailer (my parents were a bit skeptical about me taking on such a responsibility). But finally they came around and supported my decision since they were so thrilled that I had changed from a bar-room brawler to a Bible-toting Christian. They were totally convinced something wonderful had happened and said "Amen!"

-----But the best was yet to come!!!----

One night I took JoAnn and Mary (ages 3 and 6) to a church revival. That night I told Brother Hurst, "I know I'm saved and things are going great, but something is missing. He prayed for me. After the service we headed home. On the way, it seemed the Lord brought to my remembrance an incident that had happened years before my God-drawn conversion. We had been partying, drinking, drugging, etc, on a little beach in Bayside, TX. I had a little boat that me and J.B. had built (a red, all wood, flat-bottom boat). It wasn't real big but it was heavy. At one point I ended up on that boat by myself. Everybody else was up on the shore. I kind of panicked when I realized it was almost dark and I was pretty high and I was drifting out into the bay. Everybody thought that was pretty funny, but it wasn't. I could have ended up all night drifting to who knows where. When that dawned on me, I grabbed the anchor and threw it in---guess what? It wasn't tied on to the boat's rope!! I only had one option---I grabbed the rope and jumped in the water that came just below my chest. I began the long, arduous task of pulling that boat back to the shore which took about what seemed hours. But finally I made it to the shore. Everybody got a big laugh out of that. As I was thinking about that experience going up on the 13th block of N. Ave. D that night, it was like God said, "that boat was all those sins I have forgiven you for" ----then I saw God cut the rope!! I was free from that great enormous weight, and friend, I went nuts!!! It was a rush I had never experienced!! I took the girls home and told my wife what had happened and that I had to find brother Hurst and let him know too. I went by my parent's house and literally burst in and told them that something wonderful had happened!! I think they thought I was on drugs, drunk or just gone crazy again. Next morning I was still filled with that wonderful anointing that has never, to this day, subsided.

Well, forty-two years have come and gone and I've been blessed with 3 children of my own. I've been through many trials including my wife's death in 1996 of leukemia.

Then in 1998 God blessed me with Linda, and life has never been better!! Old things passed away forty-two years ago, and all things just keep getting newer!!!

Table of Contents

Poems with a Purpose—Life with a Cause

By David P. Carlson

This book was written for one purpose and one purpose only, which is for you to view your life behind, yet through this thin veneer of words and phrases, stories and allegories, all created to blend from within, (you the reader) personal considerations of specific recollections of times, (ill or well spent) - but now content to attempt to climb above your future's considerable mountains of compilations. These poems (as is life itself) without a purpose or a point are as trees without limbs or leaves, no trunk or bark, no roots or seeds to grow, could never become a shade for that next generation—please attempt to read, then bask in some related truth—Take a mental sabbatical and say, "That's what I'll do for the rest of my days"—and so is the fruit of enlightenment of so many trees of truth—all within your reach upon heaven's special ladders—each rung a book, each step a gate that swings forever wider, so as to view the world around and your place in life, three-score and six rungs higher.

Shadow Man and the Poet's Pen

By David P. Carlson

Poetry, a series of written events all conspiring to force the reader
to recall a multitude of people, places and things so remote
(yet so greatly inhabited by the beauty of so many painful events)
that they so unwillingly paint a portrait of themselves so vivid
that reality yields to the divine awareness of a conscious serenity,
so complex that all (so simply put) are sadly mundane;--

Unforeseen and suddenly this solitary life burst upon the scene,
confronts the risings in his mind, then kneels to the descending
light of time and grace, affirms the course, then steps across the
line so quickly drawn;--

With a stuttering gasp and a choking hiss, he speaks the words,
"Amen, so be it, so now it is". Now truth has been revived as it
comes to light in one dark corner of his mind: there beneath the
shadowed veil now reveals a man couched and pale, clad in a coat
of mail; content to shun the light of the poet's pen. So now he
stands, now to embrace the waiting hope for a life well spent, all
within the realm of the poet's spin on a life within, never to be
content to die again, all propelled by the tip of the poet's pen—
Amen.

A Dreamer of Dreams

By David P. Carlson

Dreams, tangled and snarled, unraveled and crushed, all are reduced to a cloud of thick swirling dust. Now dreams are just dreams, each one bears our trust, that disparaging moments must come with the pains of offence through the deeds of mistrust—Both life and love have a marvelous way, to clutch, then embrace each day with a hug, called the veracity touch. So simple to dream, but to awake, that's hard to endear, for from there our ways are so painfully clear. No fog or smog, no smoke or debris can obscure forever the sight of the risk of a place called tomorrow, the now, or today. So stand to the task, then breathe a deep breath of cold frigid air—plunge headlong through the snow crust and ice, to the depths of the lake of gloom and despair. Now ascend with new hope to the surface above, as you lunge with each stroke, for a fresh breath of love—Now though numb, but fully awake, you see the work to be done. Now unravel the tangles, the doubts and mistrust, of the life you've imagined from the dawn of your youth to your twilight at dusk. There is only one thing, and hope you'll agree, that your dreams are your own unless you give them away—Now a dream is just a dream, a poem or a scheme, it could go either way—so look up to your Maker, bow and then pray—Lord grant my dreams to be immersed in the light of your will every day.

After Death

By David P. Carlson

With eyes of fear, with the mind of his life before him, a man screams into death's arms-he hears, he sees, he believes hell is upon him- To cry, to scream, to clutch his body, to fall, to roll, to fling wasted words upon a Godly fate are not there to be had- Death is silent as an empty room. For four lifetimes he exists as if in animation. With a shriek as his dying breath he hears his name- his fear twice-fold, no one sees except darkness- he moves without earthly sensation- a speck then lightens the horizons of eternity- Light so bright he is not and he has darkness in the light, the light of a million meteors, of a million suns,- not one of a million lifetimes of word phrases, of genius minds, none could describe the chill of death's promise- The warmth that flows as saints in brilliant exuberance, the evolving eternities which saturate his being, melts his soul pure——blossoms heaven into full bloom. Without sin he faces Lord God Almighty, for without sin his face unveils before him. His love spirals universal motion, eternal Godness takes all for sanity, speaks for a jubilant deliverance——THE GARDEN OF EDEN IN MAN'S ONCE AGAIN—— In that land of unknown sadness he feels the chill of another death promised hour-his name rings again a million bells as his life spills from around him- he feels gravity as his first life would describe- "The battle of my soul!" he cries inside, but "No!", judgment has been pasted! The battle of his soul rages on-his gravity jerks as ocean waves in the midst of the savior's light- then appears the darkness-spots-dots-big-small-enormous-in each one he knows his sin. Words and dots dim the light; the light becomes darkness, then a steady ringing. MAN MUST BE SHOWN HEAVEN-MAN MUST BE SHOWN HELL-HE MUST KNOW WHAT HE IS MISSING.

Ambrosia——_a poetic concept of the drug world of Texas, USA and Beyond_

(Webster: Ambrosia-the food of the gods)

By David P. Carlson

I sat alone in a little boat in the midst of a chocolate sea. As I faced the west the eastern sky lends her morning light to stream her beams across the vast expanse, there to bathe the cotton-candy clouds with a bright vermillion glow as they hovered low against those caramel-covered mountain peaks. Then, there descending swiftly to the valleys fog-enshrouded coast, I saw the eagles swooping low to view the land, then soaring up to their mountain nests, high above the silhouettes of countless mountain homes. There amidst the flowing meadows of green and yellow gold was a little gingerbread church house with its pepperminted steeple towering up above the road below. I saw trees like men marching down in rows, through the hollows, and honeycomb-like trails to a vale of towns called Royal Garden Grove in the county of Ambrosia. Now rising high in the morning's frosty glow, marshmallow creams and puffs join together, then separated above the hills into the sky. Like Christmas cookies they break, then scatter, sprinkling sparkling glitter, like fireflies upon the limbs of the towering oaks, those giant sequoias and cypress groves, growing up out of the cherry sno-cone river's valley, and don't forget their friends the pines. This majestic sight of hills and trees imbedded in the rocks and leaves, soaked with light beneath the sky of coconut blue, sparkling like snow and ice;

(Next)

then transformed to produce the mood for a silent gaze upon the forest's fallen timbers, their friends, the faithful few, their stories lost, never to be told—only time can change their minds to what was really true. Now that's about the gist of it, my gentle, sweet, seabreeze friend, that sweeps across this chocolate lake, where there within your caps are frosted purest white, with a tint of gold from that banana pudding sun so bright, so bright she drips her residue of golden rays, raining drops like jelly beans on lemon pie like waves that splash, then swirl and then emit a savor as sweet as vanilla jelly in the chocolate pudding waves of a hurricane. Now for this massive literary flood, (like syrup flowing on my plate of words) the ocean sprays her angry waves upon my mast and sails of white and sugar glaze. Pepperminted oars slap the waves that take our boat forever closer to the shore. Now content I now relent to drive her bow into the brown and white sugar sand, "the shore of Ambrosia". Now stroll we may my sweet tooth friend beneath the palms, trees like lollypops of iceee green, oozing candy nectar from her dangling dates of blue and red to feed her friend the hummingbird, hovering there above her limbs she stretched to extend her syringe-like stem, in to draw the strength into her soul within—Now where is this place you intend to go, there within your mind, your island home of honeycombs without the bears and bees.

(Next)

Those combs that drip of dreams of your every whim that you have never ever to have yet to let unfold—where is this place where life and peace means life is sweet along those rocks and candy cliffs, with its ice cream shallow slippery shoals. What is the sweetest thing you could ever taste? Could it be God's manna so described, small as "hoar frost or coriander seeds, baked sweet as vanilla coated wafers to bring you peace, to appease your craving life, to amaze those taste buds you've come to trust, to steer you clear of the bitter winter's cold and tears---or does this scenario compute to you as just like your overrated, yellow-brick road that leads to the Land of Oz. Do you really want to be a lifetime member of the lollypop gang of yesterday? that never is and never was? Remember those trees towering high in the morning's light, so tall and strong, hiding from view the smallest tree of all, the Tree of Life and also there that royal honeycomb that drops of royal jelly, that only kings and queens are allowed to enjoy if they ever expect to be adorned with the royal robe of eternal life, and then permits you to partake of God's smorgasbord of sweets galore? So now we have within our grasp this treasure map (here upon this special island shore) that shows the way to the greatest treasure to have ever been amassed, "God's hidden manna" that comes only by one simple act of your own submission to the Son of a holy God and his salvation—all it takes is faith and just one bite of this royal fruit from this tree of Life, but this time with God's final and complete permission.

A Moment in Hell

By David P. Carlson

No place to repent—no tears,

No reviling accusations,

Only a figure's motions so emote as depicting the
revolving of a continual burning;

As molten drops on tender skin,

Devised to absorb the sizzling,

Then transformed to immediate regeneration;

Only the sound of the revolving kiln,

Till millions and millions of years reveal,

Only a moment has gone by in Hell.

Aplomb

By David P. Carlson

Plastic flowers upon the throne, blue and pink,

White and yellow—solid rock the back drop.

Fields of green and hidden seeds spreading their leaves,

Gathering in life-giving rain,

Igniting the life within the stem,

Transforming the flowers face into a grin—

Colors bloom in a sea of green—

Blue sky, a fresh back drop.

Flowers swoon in gentle winds,

True and free upon the throne.

God spreads the grass with gold as glass

Upon the face of man,

Now aplomb, the Life of Grace—

No place for plastic's taste,

Only Life upon the golden throne.

Biblical Poem by Holy Spirit—

Scriptural Arrangement by David P. Carlson
Psalm 105:13,14,15,16,23,34,39,41,42,43,45

13) They went one nation to another, 14) He suffered no man to do them wrong, 15) saying touch not mine anointed and do my prophets no harm; 16) Moreover he called for a famine, he break the whole staff of bread, 23) So Israel came into Egypt and sojourned in the land of Ham, 34) He spoke and the locusts came and caterpillars without number to devour the fruit of the ground—39) He spread a cloud for a covering and a fire to give light in the night. 41) He opened the rock and the water gushed out, 42) For he remembered His holy promise 43) to bring forth his people with joy, 45) that they might observe his statutes, and there to praise the Lord.

Biblical Poem by Holy Spirit II—

Scriptural Arrangement by David P. Carlson
Psalm 147:16; 149:4, 147:17-18, 148:8, Proverbs 2:10, 3:8, 3:35

Psalm 147:16-- He giveth snow like wool: he scattereth the
hoarfrost like ashes.

Psalm 149:4-- For the LORD taketh pleasure in his people: he will
beautify the meek with salvation.

Psalm 147:17-18-- He casteth forth his ice like morsels: who can
stand before his cold? He sendeth out his word, and melteth them:
he causeth his wind to blow, and the waters flow.

Psalm148:8-- Fire, and hail; snow, and vapours; stormy wind
fulfilling his word:

Proverbs 2:10-- When wisdom entereth into thine heart, and
knowledge is pleasant unto thy soul;

Proverbs 3:8-- It shall be health to thy navel, and marrow to thy
bones.

Proverbs 3:35-- The wise shall inherit glory: but shame shall be the
promotion of fools.

Bloom Again

By David P. Carlson

A poem or a song, they bloom for a moment
And then they're gone.
Then they spring to life when a problem is solved—
The tune and the song now so much alive.

By chance your world has gone sadly awry,
And your goals in life seem in the sky.
Jot it down, that rhyme or that tune;
In time it might come true.
And even if it dies and fades away
The hope is then that it will bloom again
Some pale and sunless day.

Boston

by David P. Carlson

Slivers of glass in coagulating blood, drips then drops from folding chairs with aluminum frames; twisted limbs, severed and scattered, just another passing glimpse from the rear-view mirror of days gone by of terror and sorrow.

Teepees with numbers mark the locations of shells and their casings, as murder and rage collect the raves of the citizen's gaze on the evening's latest news-worthy sensations;

Chanel eight, ten and eleven providing instructions on iphones and other informational connections; all broadcasting precise details down to the last intricate switch, and the bombs best location to enhance the blast for tomorrow's presentation for their products and their commercials—all clad around the past days of gore and destruction---all guaranteed to stampede the market to financial success as citizens watch the times subside and compress,

Then for a moment of silence, they reluctantly pause for these unfortunate few, these victims of chance, all laid to rest in their final location;   placed neatly between the "best life insurance around", to "how to lose weight", or "what to take when pain abounds"; Super Bowl Sundays or baseball World Series can never compare to the world's sponsors of terror or their profits from despair.

Cleanse the Land

By David P. Carlson

How clever to supply the tenants of this old ball of dirt

with hand-me-downs and tyrants frowns,

Then they pass around the shovels, the picks,

And also sticks to start a fire on this hallowed ground called
home.

So low beneath the walls and towering halls of Justice,

Lies "Old Glory", tired but true.

So once again the acts of man has quaked the land

And moved the tides to higher ground thus the flooded land.

Acts of God or acts of man?

Or is it just a simpler plan to cleanse the land and dispel

the man.

How clever. How sad.

Clouds

By David P. Carlson

Bulging white to towering heights these cumulus giants piling up, then spreading wide as a mountain range of ice and matter, charged with nature's natural currents of a mind alive—now bursting forth as winds arise; these morning rays delight the sky with the dawn of awaking eyes. So a day in this life has now begun, this conscious mind soars to heights of stratocumulus design. Layers of altocumulus, fleecy globular cloudlets roll in gold in the morning light, completes the whole of this vast domain—this winter day—so dark, so gray. Frantically, the sky descends to a nimbostratus state, as tears of cumulostratus yesterdays confirms the shades of dark and gray, sadly joy has slipped away; so as the rain depicts the shame, so the sun drapes the horizon of altostratus clouds with a brilliant fringe of yellow gold, so low, then fades to shades of yesterday—so young, yet so old. Creeping in with gold in hand, such are the thoughts of cirrocumulus, with hand in hand her sister cirrostratus, together they roam to heights unknown—with the shock of un-natural joy their attitude commands the wind to rise to heights of trato-cirrus altitudes; with their minds deprived of precious air they skip across the fields of the cirrus icy plains, there to view the faceless forms of countless cumulus clouds of kin. Now, so far below, life reminds me once again, I must descend to a nimbus form, a shining cloud , then expel the rain to feed the fields of the earth below. This nimbus circle, this halo of grace with its cumulonimbus throne sits one and one alone. Peering down from above the clouds, he sees the approach of the death of life as we now know. Now high above the dome of the highest of the cirrus fields of crystal ice; the heavens shiver in the cirrus stratosphere at the thought that one soul could be left behind to view the disappearing clouds above, to be replaced by fire and a life alone. Now decompress, descend again to the land below, ponder life and God alone; prepare each day as the scriptures say— Isaiah 44:22 (KJV) "I have blotted out, as a thick cloud, thy transgressions and as a cloud. thy sins return unto me. For I have redeemed thee."

15

The Message

<u>Clouds</u>

By the Holy Scriptures of the King James VISION of the Bible (scripture arrangement by David P. Carlson)

Taken up by a cloud (Jesus) Acts 1:9 — Arrived in heaven on a <u>cloud</u> the <u>same day</u> as prophesied in 588 BC (Daniel 7:13)—Last days foretold by Jesus—Mark 13:26; Matt. 24:30; Rev. 1:7 by John

Acts 1:9 *(after crucifixion and resurrection and moments before ascension) and when he had spoken these things, while they beheld, he was taken up; and a cloud received him out of their sight.*

Daniel 7:13-14-*I saw in the night visions, and, behold, one like the Son of man came with the <u>clouds</u> of heaven, and came to the Ancient of days, and they brought him near before him. And there was given him dominion, and glory, and a kingdom, that all people, nations, and languages, should serve him: his dominion is an everlasting dominion, which shall not pass away, and his kingdom that which shall not be destroyed. (Same day-moments after ascension)*

Acts 1:10-11-*And while they looked steadfastly toward heaven as he went up behold, two men stood by them in white apparel; Which also said, Ye men of Galilee, why stand ye gazing up into heaven? this same Jesus, which is taken up from you into heaven, shall <u>so come in like manner</u> as ye have seen him go into heaven. (before His crucifixion, resurrection, and ascension)*

Mark 13:26-*And then shall they see the Son of man coming in the clouds with great power and glory.*

Matthew 24:30-*and then shall appear the sign of the Son of man in heaven: and then shall all the tribes of the earth mourn, and they shall see the Son of man coming <u>in the clouds</u> of heaven with power and great glory.*

Revelation 1:7--*Behold, he cometh <u>with clouds</u>; and every eye shall see him, and they also which pierced him: and all kindreds of the earth shall wail because of him.*

<u>Common</u>

By David P. Carlson

Common is the man beneath the clouds of power,

Obscure is the view from the sons of scorn,

Rejected is the seed of God in the tilling hands of man,--

But in the midst of the mist a liquid gives rain

To praise and simple worship.

Beneath the toiling sod a Godly breath gives life to death

And all that is common becomes complex,

Thus the Birth of an Uncommon Man, too

Spans again with his own hand the future home of the

Tree of Life, far from common,

But Truly Blessed and Born-Again!!

Cornucopia—Oil Patch of Plenty

By David P. Carlson

Triple digits within the blackened crust of oil and gas we've come to trust. Tip-tap, tip-tap—a sonic blast to jar the tar, to release the earth's cemented grasp, to increase the checks and balance acts. These hearts, (that dream of this treasured liquid ore beneath the ground and mounds of flowing royal oil), they pound the beat, then churn and scream, "relief, relief!!" for the common cold of frigid air between the folds of man's old and tattered pocketbooks, with those cancelled checks and debts galore.

Now there within the earth we hear the wailing moans and groanings (sometime it seems out of control) to contain that cornucopia horn of plenty, immersed in the blackened gold in those far away seemingly unreachable places of the catacombs of prehistoric forest creatures. Those painful blisters sometimes arise upon man's hands and then within their souls. But all is never lost if all those riches gained can increase the praise of the one that left them there---so deep, so deep, but just within our grasp that slippery treasure chest to finance the truth, if only for one soul to find his way to the fields where dreams are drilled each and every day, -- there to produce a fresh supply of anointing oil for all that have gone astray.

Details and the Master Craftsman

By David P. Carlson

Details, the invisible flaws in every life

And law pertaining to all that seek perfection.

With a craftsman's skill he avoids the pain

Of starting over again.

His success over a momentary failure of the slightest
minute detail requires all his master status to repair the
hair-line crack in his monumental fracture.

But, alas, he cries as he finishes his task,

"That's just the way I planned it!"

Elapsed Time

David P. Carlson

Time is short, eternity is forever.

Counsel your heart,

Bemoan the past insurrections.

The distance is rolled and framed

In the Lord's memory past—

Yet eternally grasped.

Forever time and space have tasted grace,

Forever concealing the day when time elapsed.

First Dawn-First Night: The Dayspring of Creation

By David P. Carlson

From darkness streams a beam of light across the horizons of a new creation—the dayspring dawn creates the shadows from the mountain's peaks to the chirping sparrows, fluttering and shaking off the morning's dew, cleansed and dried by gentle winds, their songs fly high to paint the sky with their melodies of living nature.

The mournful cooing of a lonely dove consoles the moment as time stands still; there from the shadows the chill between the valleys and the hills rejoice in warmth as the rays arise with a brilliant flash, with a torrent rush, the towering clouds emerge, burst into a glorious white from the Master Fuller's touch—the light ascends to slash the sky, to confront the day; as a gust of wind bathes the forest and the lake—the pine trees blink, then come awake to greet the day.

With darkness now dismissed, the Ancient of the Ages controls the mist. The garden path now leads the way, etched with flowers and their petals to define the patterns, the colors and their shades— "The garden of Miss Eden" , if you may.

No man to stroll and search the caves, only the spirit of preparation divides and guides the land to its final destination—the sun sinks, then fades away—for as a day, this day is as no other.
The Day star prepares to make His way into the night, prepares to shine and give His light to that first night of the One and only First Begotten, Dayspring Day.

Golden Rays

By David P. Carlson

Back road country sunshine hunkered down above the clouds,

Peering down from time to time,

Then dark clouds dominate the sky,

The rain and hail abuse the news of clearing skies,

Rabbits scurry too their holes,

Only to find there a "no entry" sign

Floating upon the rising slides of mud from a

Back creek's stormy summertime.

But in a moment the clouds do break,

So enters in once more again for Nature's sake

Back road country sunshine.

Abundant are God's golden rays, His back road country sunshine.

Guitars, Cars and Butterflies

By David P. Carlson

Guitars, cars and butterflies, all symbols of a life
inside,

Engaged in strife, but strings fly high,

All notes caressed by sweet evening's air

As a child at play, his motor sounds with rage

Around the wooden floors.

With hand in charge, The Car,--

Outside the race is always on,

Colors slash the sky,

The child, He'll catch a butterfly,--

All symbols of a Life inside;

Guitars, cars, and butterflies.

Here I Go Again

By David P. Carlson

Verse 1

I once knew a man who told me about Jesus.

He told me about a life beyond the grave.

He told me what this Jesus meant to him, then He told me
friend, "You've gotta get born again."

I said now there he goes again, talkin' about this Jesus,

There he goes again, talkin' about his very special love.

So as I watched him as he walked down life's rugged road,

I said now there he goes again, talkin' about his soul.

Verse 2

Now the years have come and gone, I filled my life with sin.

The life I thought was new, well it's all old again.

But I remembered what that man said, about how you gotta
get born again,

Oh here I go again, I'm worried about my soul.

I said, now there I go again, worried about this Jesus,

Here I go again worried about my very, very soul.

So as I walked just right on down life's rugged road,

I said now here I go again, I'm worried about my soul.

Verse 3

Now I believe the hand of God touched my life that night,

While down on my knees, there in deep despair.

Well it wasn't too long from then, well,

Praise God I was born again.

Oh, here I go again, praising my dear Lord.

I said, now here I go again, talking about my Jesus.

Here I go again talking about his very precious love.

So as I walk just right on down life's rugged road, well,

Here I go again—you gotta get born again,

I said, here I go again, Jesus saved my soul!

Here Today—Gone Tomorrow

By David P. Carlson

*Comfortably dreaming of the last passing days of consoling
the hours of desperate decisions now tucked neatly away—
Thoughts like streams of Biblical-like lights peering into the
blackness of those compromising cracks; slowly consoling the
acts of the past; flash the bulb; "Are you here today?"—*

*Reality bursts upon the scene; the preacher hastens to crack
the shell around the thoughts that swell beneath the
shimmering bell of man's golden dome of sanity,*

*"Are you here today?" are you not content to amend one last
thought or just disappear to the end of that flying spear of
eternity's constant risings, then descend above and then
below that morning's special message to you and all there
within the pews, "Are you here today?"*

"Yes, I am, but maybe not aware—how can I say?"

*With the preacher's decision now set in stone, he drapes the
congregation with one final blow, "I have one last
confession, I pray your forgiveness will atone,
If you're here today, tomorrow this place may or may not be
your home.*

Hot Rods and Lincolns

by David P. Carlson

Verse 1(Chorus)

I got a hot rod and a Lincoln, a little blonde and a bag of gold,

That don't mean that the Lord don't love me

And I'm gonna go and lose my soul,

'Cause everything I got ya know belongs to Him,

If He wants it He can have it back

'Cause my "hot rod" is linkin' up to the Glory Train.

Verse 2

Elijha's ride was a chariot of fire when he left the world that day,

Spokes were a-smokin' like a mighty locomotive,

But through it all you could hear him say,

"I'm leavin' this world and I ain't comin' back,

Oh, but maybe for the Judgment Day,

I got a hot rod that's a linkin' up to the Glory Train.

Verse 3

Now Isaiah spoke of a glorious train that filled the temple that day

Maybe not a locomotive

But it still was a token of our Lord and Savior Christ and King.

Now if you're goin' slow and you need a little "go",

Let the Holy Ghost power your ride,

Then your hot rod will be linkin' up to the Glory Train.

Chorus

I got a hot rod and a Lincoln, a little blonde and a bag of gold,

That don't mean that the Lord don't love me

And I'm gonna go and lose my soul,

'Cause everything I got ya know belongs to Him,

If He wants it He can have it back

'Cause my "hot rod" is linkin' up to the Glory Train.

Verse 4

Now the Glory Train is a mighty fine ride to sail through heaven someday,

It won't be smokin' so we won't be chokin' on that heavenly air inside,

The rails will be gold and stories will be told on the corner of Glory and Main,

About the hot rods that are linkin' up to the Glory Train.

Chorus

I got a hot rod and a Lincoln, a little blonde and a bag of gold,

That don't mean that the Lord don't love me

And I'm gonna go and lose my soul,

'Cause everything I got ya know belongs to Him,

If He wants it He can have it back

'Cause my "hot rod" is linkin' up to the Glory Train.

Ice World

By David P. Carlson

*Shave the ice, reveal the Holy scriptures so concealed in diverse
layers of polluted waters, then frozen by years and years of
merging versions, all adapted to slice and dice the words and
phrases of this world's best-seller into a multi-million dollar profit.
Twice, then thrice, then multiplied till the words are so divided
that to recognize the sound of such poetic bliss is like hearing the
songs that David sang and played to Saul above a serpent's hiss in
the dark corner of the forest—wholly unrecognizable is the Holy
Scripture's caress of the songs and psalms that guide your path
from behind such a subtle and shadowed foreboding mask. The
ghost of this nation's once holy tenet was that one emerging
version is in fact God's one and only letter to this Christian
nation. These scribes that labored in King James' vineyard, so
guided by God's Holy Spirit to produce a literary fruit of the vine
still needs no corrections. This Word of God, the Holy Bible is not
a simple version, but God's solon; not to be transcended, striped or
frozen beneath the oblique towering slabs of ice before our eyes.
Shave the ice, subdue the lies that proclaim that wisdom comes
from a man's demand for subtle change thus counterfeits His Holy
Name known as "The Word" thus proclaimed; their end then is to
induce a venom so diverse as to confuse from verse to verse the
total truth. Return to the King of King's holy vision and
projections better known as the King James Version.*

In Jesus Precious Name

By David P. Carlson

On our knees we've knelt around these altars here,

And the prayers we've prayed, we know our God, He hears.

As tears are shed from within our eyes, we've said,

"These things we ask in Jesus' precious name".

It's like our tears glowed crimson red in God's eternal flame,

Then were consumed with His love for Jesus' precious name.

I know sometime, somewhere, I know my mother prayed;

On bended knees through tears I hear her plea;

"Dear God above, one more chance for his soul to believe,

This thing I ask in Jesus' precious name.

It's like her tears glowed crimson red in God's eternal flame,

Then were consumed in His love for Jesus' precious name.

As storm clouds roll through Gabriel's last solo.

As earthquakes shake and our sun turns black as coal.

As fangs from hell sink deep in each man's soul,

Then no more chance to call on Jesus' precious name.

Lord, in Jesus' precious name, draw back the veil,

Let mercy's truth proclaim Thy coming reign,

Then maybe one more chance for the world for Jesus' precious name.

It's like our tears glowed crimson red in God's eternal flame,

Then were consumed in His love for Jesus' precious name.

In the Morning

By David P. Carlson

In the morning, in the evening,

And when the skies are lit by the rays of the setting sun.

I think about Lord Jesus and how he came like a dawn upon this earth,

How He rose up in the sky like our noon-day sun on high,

How He set His life to be on that cross for you and me,

And how, if we should live and die without Jesus by our side,

Well, then we've seen the last of the setting sun.

But I'm so glad to know that my God has let me know,

That the sun though set will dawn upon the morn,

And I'm so glad to show that my God has let me know

That He set His son on Calvary and if I'll believe he'll rise in me,

Just to let this whole world know

That the sacrifice was made, and the price for sin was paid,

And if we should die enslaved, then all is night,

Where Eternity has prepared a place absent of Light,

Absent of Grace,

Where never again to see the Face of the morning's gift,

Of the Dawn of Day!

It's Never Over

By David P. Carlson

Squinting eyes behold the setting sun behind the darkened clouds,
the gray and black of the rolling hills and fading meadows.
The silent breeze beneath the trees become broken
by falling leaves and nocturnal creatures.
The cold and frigid winds assure you that it's over—
the day almost gone, your eyes are slowly closing;
then there within your mind the sun is slowly rising,
the voice speaks as echoes within the canyons of your mind.
Beneath the pain the Son of a creating being still holds that moment,
that desperate cry from years gone by,
there in the springtime of that youthful season when,
"I believe, please come on in, forgive my sin",
these echoes from years before simply say,
"Rise and hold the sun from falling freely,
from disappearing into the abyss of tomorrow's yesterdays.
The light of that seemingly lost salvation once again holds still,
there once again to illuminate the day,
to eclipse the cold in that endless maze.
The light once again a welcome friend, once again in the morning's
light, with a gentle tap upon your shoulder,
He then bends down, speaks in your ear---
"Enjoy the light my dear and know it's never over."

Life Unfettered—Time Left Behind

By David P. Carlson

Time and life crossed the line together,
It's what they deliver on the other side that makes the
difference.

Time excels, life feels compelled to bridge the gap
between the cavern and the hills—time cradles life
but life forever struggles to break the hold and resists
the urge to dodder beneath the heavy load of the gifts
of life from Jesus and His father.

Hand in hand they come as one to step up to the line,
they make amends, then say goodbye;
and though betrothed since time began,
one must stay behind.
For across that line time can never go—
for in that place life is never fettered—
always free to roam.

Lily Fields

By David P. Carlson for Linda Carlson

Touch this flower child,

Touch her golden hair,

Favor her in purest white,

Give to her her sight,

Let her take what her heart finds golden,

Only she will know.

I feel I have touched a garden's gift,

A love in lily fields,

A flower untouched,

A woman held enchanting.

Lost

By David P. Carlson

A trembling Fawn was left unknowing and pale, and compelled to search for refuge in the winter gardens.

His coat (bleached by thickets, brush fields, tall trees that let in blankets of filtered light), shivers in his shadowy world.

The beauty of mothers and thankful phrases blessed his path and led him home.

Man-Woman: Castles Made of Sand

By David P. Carlson

Gentle winds wash the sand ashore, then curls, then burrows beneath the rocks and turtle shells; as the ocean breathes the waves contract, then howl retreat to the perpetual pounding fleet of a million waves to shore; then again to coil and strike the helpless hoards of minute life there upon that shore. With the disappearing sun, the moon and tide arrive on time to see the gentle winds transformed to a raging storm of foaming, liquid hate, then bursts the gates of man's advance to control the beast of time and weight. Heavy on the heart of man is to lie in peace upon the shore—As a sea of shells upon the shifting sand, man lies within the path of the waves of Hell. There within his castle made of sand, he ignores the roar, bows his head and calmly shuts the door.

Without God's plan a man is just this castle made of sand, washed by waves and the winds of time, forever buried as a life disguised there beneath the rising tide—man—this castle made of sand that was never meant to die, but forever meant to live again as a lighthouse, there within his castle make of sand.

Motif

By David P. Carlson

The temple so decked and domed with the tenet that all that
ascend like scrolls are as a motif of all that bow beneath
such a lofty structure—

Truly they are as pilgrims setting foot ashore at the base of
that mighty EDIFICE, mounting up to touch the mortar
between the stones—

Amazed they read the Ancient Scrip, flashing back at times
as a tirade of rules and symbols, then come crushing through
the temple of man's imperfect structure, dissolved by the
magnificence of it all;

Then left to caress the Golden Rules etched upon the face of
the temple's golden dome—

Left to sacrifice their own eternal souls there beneath those
mighty stone towers, there their groans, their shame, their
names, as a motif—for such is the art of such a brutal
regime. In a land far away they chant a name; they cry and
sing, but all is muted by the fluttering of angel's wings high
above the earth's own crystal dome.

God sees, He understands the grief of lost souls untold,
shamefully all in the name of death and pain beneath that
Golden Dome.

News Flash

By David P. Carlson

Commonly reported is the severity of a common misconception that the current public opinion has turned unanimously to various forms of veracity (which now has an evil connotation, mainly that) the once highly regarded altruism (which now in fact is also considered a profitable act of kindness with long-term consequences of major discontent and discomfort), and that this misconception is absolutely without basis, and that such allegations should be immediately extracted from all public media——the latest polls do show that the public's consciousness now confirms that nearly all, if not everybody loves to view a good TV crime now and then, and then feels ecstatic about not being locked up for cheering on the criminal and his antics. We all truly, with all sincerely hope and pray that this law breaker would be genuinely rehabilitated by the end of his sentence, to be regarded worthy to be free and clear, and so elevated, even to the point that his name would be celebrated in the arenas of the world as a man of renown, a citizen of repute, who now has been revitalized, rejuvenated and rejoined to his former ministerial practice of altruism, so then to become a true bearer of active kindness, without charge or disregard of veracity.

No Right to Be Defeated

By David P. Carlson

Up on a hill two thousand years ago, they planted an old, dead tree. Some people thought that the wood would rot, and old Satan would claim the victory. But not so, not so, not so, not so, not so, cause...

Up on the cross Jesus died for the cause of the lost, beat, defeated man. And it wasn't by chance that He died upon the branch of the tree at Calvary. For the God of man had a divine plan, to spring roots down from that old tree. Little did the Devil know that the tree would grow into one Eternal Victory!

We've got no right to be defeated, I said, we got no right to be defeated, since Jesus paid the price.

When down from the cross they wrapped Jesus in a cloth and they laid Him in an old, dark tomb; with a rock for a door, they all thought for sure that He'd be there forevermore. But two thousand years later, ya know, we all gather and celebrate that third day, when the rock rolled away and the price was paid for one Eternal Victory!

We've got no right to be defeated, I said, we got no right to be defeated, since Jesus paid the price.

Now with the price all paid, the Lord He went away to His home in glory land. He left the Book and Spirit of the God who sent it, and promised He'd return again. Well, it's not just so simple you can put it in a thimble, but the Word is "Just believe!" From the front to the back that Bible it's a fact, come on now, praise Him for the victory!

We've got no right to be defeated, I said, we got no right to be defeated, since Jesus paid the price.

Oh Lord, Lord, help me that I should never stray from that straight and narrow highway that You lived and died to pave. With the wide road on my left, and wide road on my right, everybody looks at me says "he's in the center stripe". And as I continue on movin' up that other way, well, I just say, Jesus loved you, friend, and He wants you home someday.

We've got no right to be defeated, I said, we got no right to be defeated, since Jesus paid the price.

Old John Round

By David P. Carlson

In a little country church on a valley's hill revival fires flared in the cold night air.
But down in the town, asleep on a cot, John Round dreamed of a hell so hot that,
He awoke with sweat upon his brow. Then he rubbed his eyes and then looked around
and he thought to himself, -- "Well, I'll go down town and have a drink or two."
As he closed the door he looked up high and there up in the sky the stars just seemed so
dim in John Round's eyes; so down the path and toward the town he walked,
But then he heard a sound and he saw a light, then John Round felt a chill that night a
he saw that lighted cross there upon the hill.--- And just for a moment there he stood
and remembered back to his own boyhood, the hymns they sang about a cross He bared,
The Mother and Dad that had brought him there. And he remembered the joy of a small
small boy and he remembered that boy once was him. Like a magnet to steel it drew him
up that hill, and there, outside on the window sill, John Round heard that anointed
Word of God. That preacher preached of a love supreme, Then John's tears came down
like a mountain stream. And there outside that November night, John Round kneeled
beneath the heaven's light and there he began to pray---"Oh, Lord, Oh, Lord, I feel
conviction here—Oh, Lord, your Holy Spirit's near—Oh, Lord, I feel this urge to
kneel— Oh, Lord, I know it's You I feel.

With head in his hands that were washed from tears, which seemed to John to be his
fallen years. He heard that preacher preach loud and clear. "If there be there one outside
in sin, let him come on in and meet Jesus here. With all heads bowed,
The prayer went up from that Christian crowd. And wouldn't you know from outside in
sin, Old John Round came on in- But his head was bowed as he lifted his eyes,
'Cause there at the front he made a preacher cry, 'cause that preacher had prayed that
very day—"Lord God, ley my old Dad be saved." Well, he tried to lead him in the
sinner's prayer, but between the sobs of joy, He just couldn't spare the air---
But that old dad reached out just as if to say, "It's all right son, I know the way." –
And with that he began to pray---"Oh, Lord, I come a sinner here today—
Oh, Lord, I know the price you paid__ Oh, Lord, I'll turn away from sin, --

Oh, Lord I invite You in." Well, they praised the Lord for that answered prayer.
And then old John he stood and shared just how the Lord had brought him there.
That night old John was born again, just like me, and you, and all your friends.
But, ya know, once we all were outside in sin, until the convicting power of the
Saviour's grace called us in. So it makes you think about a window sill.
And who's there listening when the night's real still. And what you say and what you
do, just could be the key that could free a soul. When old John came his song was sin,
But when he went home he sang again and this is what he sang---

It was:

AMAZING GRACE HOW SWEET THE SOUND THAT SAVED A WRETCH
LIKE ME;
I ONCE WAS LOST BUT NOW I'M FOUND,
WAS BLIND BUT NOW I SEE.

'TWAS GRACE THAT TAUGHT MY HEART TO FEAR, AND GRACE MY
FEARS RELIEVED;
HOW PRECIOUS DID THAT GRACE APPEAR THE HOUR I FIRST
BELIEVED!!

Once Again Perigee

By David P. Carlson

Contrary to your peace of mind is the rumbling of past allegations,
Contrary to the reoccurring dreams of the fear of falling
Is the peace of mind of falling free into the depths of
Life's seemingly eternal compassion,
Then flung into a perpetual orbit around that heavenly body
of time and matter,

Simply put (time that matters), compressed and pressured till
there at last you've reached the perigee.
At last the world around stands to honor you with a
Grand Ovation, then drowned in a torrent of man's accolades
Till the gravity of it all subsides,

The drama of the moment merely slips away,
The orbit shifts only to be stretched to its outer limits of Apogee—
The cheers diminish, reduced to sighs and heads-a-waggin'
for some personal disappointment you've delighted.

Cheer up, Life is just a momentary chatter
of a long extension-ladder just before it collapses.
But remember there upon the ground the riddle of the orbit.
With time and pressure and a little luck,
you'll once again achieve the Perigee. You've come around and
returned to spin past the warmth of that heavenly body—
And once again, Perigee.

Our Silver Wings

By David P. Carlson

Our silver wings are shining in the sunlight

Sailing through the clouds to our home

There in the sky.

In this life we live, we see that day approaching,

With tender care He guides us on our way.

Our silver wings are shining in the sunlight

Sailing through the clouds to our Home

There in the sky.

As that Gate appears we see our Blessed Savior

With out-stretched arms He greets us to our new home.

Our silver wings are shining in the sunlight

Sailing through the clouds to our Home

There in the sky.

Palm Tree

By David P. Carlson

This stump that now is, once towered high unto the sky; from
there, she viewed the countless lives that paraded by.
Now herself with all her pride, now lies scattered with her day, of
fourscore and five.
A pathetic end to this majestic palm, a tree of lives all as fallen
limbs, each one remembered when the moments came for victories
won and times of pain for lives undone.
Each inch she grew all came to pass as a Mom and Dad, kids and
kin and all their close and faithful friends——all recorded and
gathered in.
The every days have now turned to years, now rights and wrongs
now swirl as currents beneath the river of toils and salty tears.
But through it all this grand old palm refused to die before her
time.
Now I sit here upon her tomb-wood stump and recall again how it
all began,——for now I see her fruit of dates have now become her
seeds of life for our children's trees, now springing up between the
leaves.
In it all now I enjoy the peace within this fruit of joy and precious
hope--for life has now once again begun to breathe on this old
stump, this grand and stately--old palm tree.

Passing Time

David P. Carlson

Curiously I glanced through my books
Of ageless alma maters,
Trembling at the faces of those gone on before,
The ones so much adored.
Time, like vines, coil around these trees of life,
So aged by ticks and tocks and months and years.
Curiously I ponder these times gone by,
Like vines that climb and wind
Till all is just commonly viewed
As simply a life just passing time
So many years ago.

Receive the Call

By David P. Carlson

No reception, no calls; a chronic state of platitude turns off the
intercoms;

Deafness filters out the words of phrases;

Maybe just a trace of a whispering breeze that persuades your days to
fade away with each morning it erases.

At the door you'll fight the urge to understand life's multitude of rules
that might filter in as words akin to a life of sin.

"Sleep on it", some may say, but more than likely your ears will hear
But then fade to only echoes within the caves of denial's hidden rooms
like tombs, there will be your silent dreams on sand-less shores by
wooden thrones whereon you'll judge what you deemed contrived as
falsetto pains, to tempt your pride, to surrender gain.

Venture in to this simple plan, remove the stones of wax and sand,
For they're there to mute your life-long cares, you're not aware.
What you hear will guide your path from life's despair to a truth that
shares its wisdom there.

Take the call, listen to the words of this poetic rhyme; there they'll
echo long within your mind; you'll hear the cheers and release the tears
as these words ring clear-- "Receive the Call".

Scrapbook

By David P. Carlson

Dice the memories of the past and present. Each sliver becomes an anachronism thrust into the future that we always thought would be well-compared to your future's dreams of being an actor, college professor, or maybe, the nation's most noted CIA director. On paper scraps (all documented by a picture) there laid so neatly within your books, the past compacts, and then reacts to the truth in varied depths of time and chance; never in chronological order. Now truly there is a true delusion that the sight of youthful joy (there within your framed conclusion) can bring a lasting glee for your present situation. Quickly it fades away as the book slams shut, now left with a ghostly presence of those fleeting days and years gone by, and then you sigh and walk away, and maybe even cry. These anachronistic insertions can only sift through so much distant, heartfelt compassion to then become the base foundation for a launching pad for your present anticipations. Though the past may assist, its only true participation is its indoctrination that you once were "alive and kicking". Now step through, skip toward the door of a world without a past, cleverly depart from the path you've trod and know that the bridge you've crossed is far behind, never to be again endured. Totally diverse this land wherein you find escape, never to be draped within the cloak of shame across the endless plains of your life's expanse to new horizons of carefree days—only God can recognize your life is more than books of scraps, but He sees the whole of your eternal soul, never to be removed, misunderstood or just forgotten there upon the shelf; there between mom's cookbooks and the Legend of Sleepy Hollow.

Second Wind

By David P. Carlson

The moment you recognize a true appreciation

Of a personal creation is the moment in life called

The joy of completion.

Only in God can your riches stand sure,

As in the moment of triumph,

Is the knowledge you've endured.

As an Olympic gold medal with its moment of fame,

All must bow down to what reality proclaims,

That the race is not over though you've crossed the line,

The truth is, my friend, life has just started

As you hear the gun sound again.

Ships Made of Tin

By David P. Carlson

Deep in the fathoms of a water rich depth,

There hidden in darkness creeps the essence of silence;

Alone in the abyss.

But finally at last the smooth,

Then jagged hills and the plains,

Of a place called the "Bottom", where all comes to rest.

Here in the Grave Yard of men and their ships

Lies once-cherished dreams of a far-away bliss,

Then only to end by the strength of the wind,

There on the bottom by their ships made of tin.

Silent Wishes

By David P. Carlson

I realized, then remembered, I saw the thought he felt,
waiting for his fellow man to stumble. He openly
wished he'd fall (a human habit of feeling joy when
another is about to go astray).

Something you know we all have said-"Oh, I wish he
would...". But if he does and we are there to see, we
look so sad, we even cry a little, and from ourselves we
hide what we really feel.

No wonder man is an embarrassed breed, for everything
we do there is someone there hoping we do it wrong.
Nothing stands that cannot be seen, and if seen it will
be criticized.

To pass the test of strength is not our goal today.
The man who feels the lowest stands beaten at his
game, there laughs are their victory cries. You will
fight again today.

"Simple Math—A Biblical Riddle"

by David Carlson

Double is the trouble, two by two.

Triple are the hardships from time to time.

Divided is the answer in a multitude of solutions.

Life concludes amidst the calculations

Just short of all the answers—

Formulated and debated to find

The problem IS the answer.

If Jesus is the Answer, then what's the problem??

So Many Years Ago

By David P. Carlson

Circuits flash, sparks, then burns,
trickles down the wrinkled frown,
seals from chin to crown.
The wrath within stored in chambers of the bones the
future plans for the offender's moans,
to soothe the pain and caress the shame that day it came--
so many years ago.

When will the venom drain away from the bones and
capillaries of the brain,
When will the sparks subside and fade away.
Will time really heal all the pain? Not so my friend.
It only leaves when the heart pumps love for that special
one that inflicted that sharp and cherished pain—
so many years ago. . . so many years ago.

Surf the Mighty Waves of Time

By David P. Carlson

She waves, then rides the waves ashore; these waves they both depict an open door. Surging deep from the ocean's floor a tremendous trembling and separation, then the door splits, then swings aside, there to pulse, push open wide, to shake the tides to create the wave she waits to ride, there upon her board. Now groaning deep within this ocean's chest (soon to birth his wave, her promised gift) a deep desire to deny her life; a story there to tell, how she rode this Dragon wave from hell. The wind and tides they both emerge, then swell then there she sees through a salty and watery glaze, this massive mountain wave projecting down with a mouth of fangs, uttering out a deep and lonesome growl———she crouches low to confront this towering, rolling wall above, this wall that howls then comes crashing down, nothing like his friends ashore, those gentle lapping waves of sorts, the ones so small that kids adore. These personifications of waves galore, they explain her moods of change, these waves that rage, then kiss the shore, then carry her to roll within the foam and then she disappears there beneath the churning sand of this dark and breathless land. This wave she rode now sinks within the deep forbidden sand, there to rejoice and then to hide until the tides arise once again———now so gently resting beneath the shifting rocks and boards, there wrapped in those snarling, seaweed strand that whipped and snapped around her tender neck. That mighty wave she rode but alas, she failed so miserably. So great a wave now roars with pride, stirs up the beds of shells, shears off the coral cliffs as if to tell, "How dare this child attempt to ride upon my bulging and foreboding neck." Waves of joy his victory cry soon subside as there he views there on high atop another towering wave, her hands held up and praising God for another amazing day. As the tempest's winds swirl and roar, attempt to drown her cry, she yells, "You may do well to rest a while, your tactics I do deplore, you mighty wave of time; but I'll be back to ride again as soon as I find my board."

Sweet Spring

By David P. Carlson

Flash, blue sky, garnished pink, her rose-petaled skies.

Corn-silk, golden clouds, sweet Spring, sweet sister of the winter.

Your voice, a morning dove, shading in spring's beginning

With dark green tones of living nature-flowers--

Freckles upon her face, green her land in morning light.

The light of day streaks bright her voices,

Over green lit forest faces peaks our golden star,

Mother Sun, Mother to all children seasons.

With all the warmth of a summer day she kisses with light the

Face of Spring,

Embraces with love this her youngest daughter—

Golden tears from mother's eyes do fall, then splash, christen gold

A white cloud scarf around Spring's pretty neck—

Sweet Spring—Sweet Spring.

Sword Master

By David P. Carlson

Crystal glass shapes the sword from diamond-tip to
golden hasp. This shaft of light is cleansed from fear by
the tempering blood from the Savior's hair. Pierced by
thorns, strained and scorned, the blood seeps through,
drips from his beard, then trickles down from chest to
loins, to the glittering sword beneath his feet;
the sword is forever meek;

Above the anvil's face the sword master's steady gaze
upon the man whose hand the sword is placed.
Crystal glass or a blade of steel, either way it's there to
wield and save the day.

Pick it up, see how it feels to grip the glass and control
the steel. Divided by the golden hasp of mercy's love,
now within the grasp of mortal man; the will to love,
the will to hate—choose love. it's not too late.

Take Charge

By David P. Carlson

Crowns and jewels line the path, then sparkling luminisent
lights light the night, condons the fading glow from crowns
of gold and precious stones—

Silently night clouds roam and block the path, leaves the
shadows to distort the dancing lights with thoughts of
doubt, thus the shell to hide within, to covet pain and
lifeless faith without—

Then the crippled faith stands and fills your hands with
rocks and tin, or is it gold?, who will know, without the
glow of proceeding light, prosperity must stand alone.

These laws of faith compel the throne to produce the charge,
to ignite your sight, to reflect the hope of jewels and gold
upon the path where you have taken flight; prosperity's
hope, the lightening bolt, cries aloud, "I receive your charge"
to take control. The only life worth the cost, is a life with
hope that has taken charge and produced a soul due jewels
and crowns and streets of gold.

The Arrival

By David P. Carlson

Christmas trips blur the years

Till songs and toys subdue the mood—

But happy are moments when the door flies open wide,

Then Mom and Dad with frantic cries shout,

"Don't run in Grandma's house!"

Those moments in a child''s rejoicing mind

Regards in time those moments of arrivals;

And then there at last there at the door,

Your mother's mother with apron on,

She smells like buns and apple pie,

And then there after a long and warm embrace,

"Hey, let's go feed the chickens!"

Now after years of countless trips,

Then there in heaven my blessed and grand arrival,

And then there at the door the God of Gods, my Savior Lord,

So sweet the savor of oils and spices; I marvel at the aroma;

Such joy sparks my response after a long and warm embrace,

"Now, let's go feed the chickens!"

The Countess and the Beast

By David P. Carlson

Searching secretly through the compost-destined

Mounds of political turmoil is the Mind-Beast,

Patented and protected by the countless conspirators,

All courting the same Countess of Courtesy,

Veiled in her transparent gown,

Naked and exposed to her own opaque arrogance

That gropes through her endless array of deceptive attires—

"Politically correct" yet completely disconnected from

All her common interests that once was "Life and Liberty",

And now she comfortably lies in the lap of all her comforters

While frolicking in the mire of her deceptiveness—

This Mind-Beast, Father to all her compulsions,

Now truly is perfidy and totally incoherent to the masses.

His mind-set is totally dedicated to his objectives

And now to us all is obviously oblique to all his surroundings
Of smoking mirrors and shouting orators.
Now hand-in-hand the Countess and the Beast in lockstep
Precision march down this stained-glass road
Where eternity's light will never shine,
Politically correct in every way,
But in his house his mirrors have forever denied his kind,
For never a reflection can ere be seen,
Because of his own opaque-crusted mind.
The Countess and the Beast now need another site
To speak their wedding vows,
Where eyes and ears are mute and blind,
Where Hate and Death can truly rhyme
Outside the sight of Truth and Love—
Transparency of another kind can only wait
By Faith, on the Other Side.

The Epic—Gold in a Coal Mine

By David P. Carlson

December 5th, 1960

Five decades and two years ago coal miners bore a heavy load,

They crossed that Guyandotte River up the Nine Mile Creek Road,

At the bottom of that stoic mountain with funeral bier well in hand.

They paused for a moment to breathe a prayer for this coal-mining man,

Then they trudged up to the top of that mountain where the cold winds blow,

And there at the top they laid his coffin down beside a six-foot deep hole.

They crossed the Guyandotte River up the Nine Mile Creek Road,

Four young girls and two brothers, Mommy had her family in tow.

They shuffled to the top of that mountain and there they cried and moaned,

For this coal-mining man they called Daddy, in their little West Virginia home

They crossed the Guyandotte River up the Nine Mile Creek Road,

And there at the top cried for their loving Daddy that wouldn't be coming hom

There beneath the trees on that cemetery's crest

That preacher bowed his head and prayed,

Said, "Lord, bless the family of William Howard Keck,

Who's coming home to You today.

He labored hard in the coal mines just to keep his family fed"

Then he paused for a moment; then he lifted his head,

Looked around and then he said,

"I can hear the cold winds blowin' down the 'hollars' and through the trees.

I can hear the lonely moaning of his life-long dreams gone by,

It's like a moonlit-night's clear sky.

Now just for a moment there in the shadows

As those cold winds swirl around the trees,

t seems I can see the spirit of William Howard Keck bowed there on his knees.

He's crossed that Guyandotte River, he's gone up that Nine Mile Creek Road,

Now his soul's up there in heaven, in God's tree-top heavenly home,

Now his story has been told. Amen.

August 18, 2012

We crossed that Guyandotte River up the Nine Mile Creek Road,

All together on top of that mountain by his hard rock tombstone.

Fifty two years have come and gone,

But his family here still knows,

William Howard Keck was a man of iron with a heart of purest gold.

Now everyone that reads these words of this solemn epitaph,

Search your soul where the cold winds blow and see where your heart is at.

Have you crossed the Jordan River, gone up Calvary's blood-soaked road?

Are you at the top of God's holy mountain where He waits for you alone?

If you're not there, just breathe a prayer, then accept His saving grace

And rise up from the "hollers" below to God's tree-top heavenly home.

In loving memory of

William Howard Keck

August 22nd, 1910 to December 2nd, 1960

"The Finger of God"

By David P. Carlson

The world is the circle upon the tip of His finger.

He counseled the motions with such a vision as torments imperfections and enforces total precision.

The world spins to the voice of His lips and orbits to the motions of His hands.

Such is the purity of His holy tempest that roars toward His unsearchable standards and rises in the fury of His judgments.

The universe folds to His countless instructions, but a moment of faith in the sight of God rejoices this Father of spirits more than the wonders of all his creations.

How marvelous is the spinning of faith upon the Finger of God!!

The Foyer

By David P. Carlson

The brothers will come if someone dies——
After the shock subsided, life returns to you alone——With your faith you abide.

Family members take advantage at every turn—even to the point of embezzlement—
After the shock has subsided, life returns to you alone—With your faith you abide.

From the song service leader the call goes out, "Greet somebody, shake hands with all
around"—

After the shock has subsided life returns to you alone—With your faith you abide.

Children are born, years return them adults, bearing empty gestures,
Shallow acknowledgements of their appreciation.
After the shock has subsided life returns to you alone—With your faith you abide.

With this life on the edge, now in sight of the end,
I now view the past atop this perilous ledge.
All of life's betrayals have now been atoned,
So life has not left me this time abiding alone—

There in the Foyer of her little church home,
God introduced me to Linda whose substance was hope
To ever be cherished and betrothed as my own.

Now life has returned this time not alone, But with a message from God, a decree from
His throne— "It's true, my son, it's not good for man to live alone,
So I sent you Linda till I call you both home. Now be true till the end and never forget
You better treat her right or you may forever regret ever being born, my friend.

Sincerely,

God

The Last Frontier

By David P. Carlson

Plunging deep through space—

Space as time folds around us,

Engulfs the mind, the spirit's soul.

Through eyes like knives,

Peering in through blood-soaked veins

and endless chains of thoughts,

Rising as a kite through the darkest night,

Then soaring through the brightest sights untold;

The Heavens, the essences of the last frontier foretold.

The Old Prayer Tree

By David P. Carlson

Paper leaves, bleached and white,
Etched with words of heart-felt grief.
These souls that bear their load of cares for their
family's tree,
compels the pen to plead the blood for hope and love.

Now, oh, Lord, to You we come, to seek for health and
strength beneath this old elm;
This holy tree by this road we trod, beckons us to seek
by faith for these leaves to be transformed to living
green, and by God's grace, we trust, redeemed.

We pray for each and every need; that all that come
might enjoy the shade beneath this old elm, this holy
tree of truth and love.

The Other Side

By David P. Carlson

Deep are the footprints in this green and rain-soaked ground--
Tenderly laid by the giants of the land-

Trudging boldly down the mountain's paths searching frantically
with clubs in hand to find the sounds at the water's edge,
That shallow lapping for a place of crossing to the other side,
To that primitive but promised land.—

Soaked and tired on the other side these giants of meer men,
Now yet small is now their stature there beneath the towering oaks
And the sequoia's massive and majestic walls of wooden faces.

The wilderness of life now lies behind, the brush, the thorns, the
stinging nettles now replaced by carpets of gleaming grass and
tender vegetation,--

Now all that lies before their eyes, the silhouettes of the towering
woods, a forest for eternal grazing
In a land of a thousand amazing graces. The land that once was
now is, that place called home at last,
Life's final destination there on the other side—
The land now lies before us.

The Ride

By David P. Carlson

As in the mind of a child this swirling vacuum of a carousel,

With music's simple rhythm;

Now it consoles the troubled tributaries leading to a place
called Anxious Anxiety,

A place of conscious relief from controlling allurements,

Blurred in the swirling emotions of songs, plus chatter,

Screams and beams of light dancing from top to bottom.

As the ride subsides and the world arrives;

The floods retreat, leave shallow estuaries of this child's
conscious mind to wonder why? Why ride?—

To complete the rhyme they're now in tune to the frantic
sounds of the world around.

Now step down to embrace the ground,

To complete the ride, so life complies,

Now enjoy the ride!

Thwarted

By David P. Carlson

Skip a rock across the pond.
Gravity lurks beneath the green and algae-laden waters.
Groping hands surge beneath this swamp of life,
Attempts to thwart the dreams within each skipping motion.
Dividing times sail above the ripples.
Songs sing the perils of each impending sinking.
Above the waters of an ocean of crashing waves is created a
tsunami of knowledge for years of weightless waiting.
Though exhausted, (but still contending that a rock might float
with the buoyancy of an ascending hope of a life hereafter),
this stone flies high and clears the pond to the land beyond.

Skip a rock, smooth and flat, across the pond;
Without fear and with faith to face the coming years,
You can now embrace your final fate to descend with grace upon
God's promise, of a bright eternal shore.
Now with thoughts of death and pain now thwarted,
Life forever more skips with hope and joy across the sand,
Now knows at last that that plan to sink and die has now forever
been (by the grace of God and His obedient Son)
Permanently and eternally thwarted.

This House of Man

By David P. Carlson

The scope of his view zooms in on this house of man,

Probes his thoughts and lays the plan

From present to the past, to the future till at last,

Tears and joy are all but salve to heal the human's hand.

His presence is drawn by a humble and contrite heart.

Overcome by mercy is every step, so the scope of His

Compassion on this house of man,

All in a moment's glance.

This Mind of Mine

By David P. Carlson

The shield is excellent as is this bone around the wrinkled moon,

Caverns host this twisted mass,

Shapings coils dart through the dented throne.

My steps crush vine and leaf-covered mats

As though ascending through the past,

The severed roots are bleeding time,

Memories now cover emerald floors derived from dying minds

And years of wasted wisdom.

Now wading to the shore, I sit, I recline,

Now severed from the "Door", the Locks that bind now open wide,

The hope of all God's endless time now lies deep within the shafts of
man's long abandoned minds,

Now free to be a kind of Liberty.

The mind in the mine, what precious ores lie buried deep

Within these wrinkled shores—

This mind of mine.

Time That Rhymes

By David P. Carlson

After the last poem has been written and the last song has been sung,

With a collection of chords that have been skillfully strung;

Together they rhyme till all that is left is a guitar in the corner

With no song to be strummed.

Now then at last, one moment at best,

One shallow breath at the beat of a drum;

Within moments his mind fully recalls,

The heart of the matter wasn't always the song,

The rhyme and the reason only reminds us in time

That the beat of the heart is the only reason for time.

The notes in Life's song that give glory to God

Can only enhance a life that's gone by.

The rhyme and the beat bring joy to the harp,

As the fingers of man play Life's lovely song—just a little too sharp.

Now all is at rest in the heart of his song,

Now the song is alive once again in the man,

So when the last chord has been strummed his soul hums along.

Whatever Your Will Be

By David P. Carlson

Whatever Your will be Lord, let it be, Lord in my life.
Whatever your will be Lord, help me daily strive.
And when there are dark clouds and sun seems not to shine.
Lord, grant me wisdom to know your will, though I seem blind.

My Lord grants me sunshine in the depths of night.
My Lord grants me springtime on those cold,
cold winter nights.
And when life seems bitter and the sweetness is all gone,
My Lord, grants me honey from the words of the Psalms.

My Lord gives me answers when my mind can't decide.
My Lord gives me freedom when those turmoils seem to bind.
And when there's a conflict and the battle rages long.
My Lord grants the victory at First Light of the Dawn.

Whatever Your will be Lord, let it be Lord in my life.
Whatever your will be Lord, help me daily strive.
And when there are dark clouds and sun seems not to shine.
Lord, grant me wisdom to know your will, though I seem blind.

Your Deeds Speak On

By David P. Carlson

1.

For every woman and man there's an hourglass of sand,

And our lives simply slip through the gates of time.

And this world simply views all your sand that's sifted through,

And your lives become a vast and an open land.

Chorus:

So let deeds speak on for the right and not the wrong

About Jesus and His plans for you and me.

Let your works be witness to what your faith in God can do,

And your life will blow as a wind across the sand.

Oh, a gospel-wind is blowin' strong—

A gospel-wind is blowin' strong across this land,

Oh Holy wind, take our hand, for all who live in Christ are born to rise again

2.

To every boy and girl it's a green and garden world,

And in time you'll view the rose beds of this world.

But gather flowers for the Lord and leave those roses and those thorns,

Lay your lilies in the hands of Christ the Lord.

Chorus:

So let deeds speak on for the right and not the wrong

About Jesus and His plans for you and me.

Let your works be witness to what your faith in God can do,

And your life will blow as a wind across the sand.

Oh, a gospel-wind is blowin' strong—

A gospel-wind is blowin' strong across this land,

Oh Holy wind, take our hand, for all who live in Christ are born to rise again

3.

Now in the wee hours of the morn our Lord and Savior wore our thorns

There upon that rugged cross at Calvary.

And that deed spoke on clear from this earth up to the throne,

Then the Father said, "It's done, Son, come on home."

2ⁿᵈ Chorus:

Oh, how that deed spoke on for the right and not the wrong.

About victory and life for you and me.

Let your works be witness to what your faith in God can do,

And your life will blow as a wind across the sand.

Oh, a gospel-wind is blowin' strong—

A gospel-wind is blowin' strong across this land,

Oh Holy wind, take our hand, for all who live in Christ are born to rise agaiᵢ